COMPASS WRITING TEST SUCCESS

COMPASS TEST WRITING PRACTICE TESTS

Note: The Compass Test is a registered trademark of ACT Inc, which is not affiliated with nor endorses this publication.

TABLE OF CONTENTS

Compass Test Information

The Compass Test in writing is a placement test that your college will administer in order to assess your writing skills. The Compass is a computer-adaptive test. This means that you will take the test on a computer and that your response to previous questions will determine the difficulty level of subsequent questions.

Test questions on the Compass Test in writing are multiple-choice. The questions ask you to look at a passage, and then find and correct errors in punctuation, grammar, mechanics, and style.

Since the Compass is a secure test, the items in this book are not actual test questions. However, this practice material is designed to simulate the difficulty level and format of questions you may face on the actual test.

Note: The Compass Test is a registered trademark of ACT Inc, which is not affiliated with nor endorses this publication.

Writing Test 1

Earthquakes

(*1*) Earthquakes have been occurring on the surface of the earth   (*2*) when there is motion in the tectonic plates in the earth's crust.   (*3*) The crust of the earth contains twelve such tectonic plates which are from four to ten kilometers in length   (*4*) when located down the sea.   (*5*) However, this on land can be from thirty to seventy kilometers long.

(*6*) Fault lines, the places where these plates meet, build up a great deal of pressure (*7*) because the plates are constantly pressing to each other.   (*8*) Although, the two plates will eventually shift or separate   (*9*) since the pressure on them is constant increasing,   (*10*) and this build-up of energy need to be released.

(*11*) When the plates shift or separate, they have an occurrence of an earthquake – also known as a seismic event.   (*12*) The point whose the earthquake is at its strongest is called the epicenter.   (*13*) In addition waves of motion, travel out from this epicenter,   (*14*) often caused widespread destruction to an area.

(15) With this likelihood for earthquakes to occur: it is essential that earthquake prediction systems are in place.   *(16)* The purpose of earthquake prediction is to give advanced warning to the population,   *(17)* with saving lives in the process.   *(18)* Yet, this prediction systems need to be reliable in order to be of any practical use.   *(19)* For this reason, scientists are currently attempting to conduct research   *(20)* on the probability of earthquakes along every of the 12 fault lines.

Writing Test 1

Item 1.

    A.   Earthquakes have been occurring on the surface of the earth

    B.   Earthquakes occurring on the surface of the earth

    C.   Earthquakes occurred on the surface of the earth

    D.   Earthquakes are occurred on the surface of the earth

    E.   Earthquakes occur on the surface of the earth

Item 2.

    A.   when there is motion in the tectonic plates in the earth's crust.

    B.   when there is motion in the tectonic plates in the earths' crust.

    C.   when there is motion in the tectonic plates' in the earth's crust.

    D.   when there is motion in the tectonic plates' in the earths' crust.

    E.   when there is motion in the tectonic plates in the earths crust.

Item 3.

    A.   The crust of the earth contains twelve such tectonic plates which are from four to ten kilometers in length

    B.   The crust of the earth contains twelve such tectonic plates, which are from four to ten kilometers in length

    C.   The crust of the earth contains twelve such tectonic plates, that are from four to ten kilometers in length

    D.   The crust of the earth contains twelve such tectonic plates, whose are from four to ten kilometers in length

    E.   The crust of the earth contains twelve such tectonic plates, where are from four to ten kilometers in length

Item 4.

    A.   when located down the sea.

    B.   when located below the sea.

    C.   when located among the sea.

    D.   when located between the sea.

    E.   when located during the sea.

Item 5.

   A.   However, this on land can be from thirty to seventy kilometers long.
   B.   However, that on land can be from thirty to seventy kilometers long.
   C.   However, these on land can be from thirty to seventy kilometers long.
   D.   However, those on land can be from thirty to seventy kilometers long.
   E.   However, them on land can be from thirty to seventy kilometers long.

Item 6.

   A.   Fault lines, the places where these plates meet, build up a great deal of pressure
   B.   Fault lines the places where these plates meet, build up a great deal of pressure
   C.   Fault lines, the places where these plates meet build up a great deal of pressure
   D.   Fault lines, the places, where these plates meet, build up a great deal of pressure
   E.   Fault lines the places where these plates meet build up a great deal of pressure

Item 7.

   A.   because the plates are constantly pressing to each other.
   B.   because the plates are constantly pressing on each other.
   C.   because the plates are constantly pressing at each other.
   D.   because the plates are constantly pressing with each other.
   E.   because the plates are constantly pressing for each other.

Item 8.

   A.   Although, the two plates will eventually shift or separate
   B.   Therefore, the two plates will eventually shift or separate
   C.   Because of the two plates will eventually shift or separate
   D.   Similarly, the two plates will eventually shift or separate
   E.   Because, the two plates will eventually shift or separate

Item 9.

   A.   since the pressure on them is constant increasing,
   B.   since the pressure on them is constantly increasing,
   C.   since the pressure constantly on them is increasing,
   D.   since the pressure on them is frequent increasing,
   E.   since the pressure frequent on them is increasing,

Item 10.

    A.   and this build-up of energy need to be released.

    B.   and this build-up of energy needs to be released.

    C.   and this build-up of energy needed to be released.

    D.   and this build-up of energy needing to be released.

    E.   and this build-up of energy is needing to be released.

Item 11.

    A.   When the plates shift or separate, they have an occurrence of an earthquake – also known as a seismic event.

    B.   When the plates shift or separate, one have an occurrence of an earthquake – also known as a seismic event.

    C.   When the plates shift or separate, we have an occurrence of an earthquake – also known as a seismic event.

    D.   When the plates shift or separate, it has an occurrence of an earthquake – also known as a seismic event.

    E.   When the plates shift or separate, he has an occurrence of an earthquake – also known as a seismic event.

Item 12.

    A.   The point whose the earthquake its at is strongest is called the epicenter.

    B.   The point where the earthquake is at its is strongest is called the epicenter.

    C.   The point at where the earthquake is at its strongest is called the epicenter.

    D.   The point which the earthquake is at its strongest is called the epicenter.

    E.   The point that the earthquake is at its strongest is called the epicenter.

Item 13.

    A.   In addition waves of motion, travel out from this epicenter,

    B.   In addition, waves of motion travel out from this epicenter,

    C.   In addition, waves of motion travel out from this epicenter

    D.   In addition waves of motion travel out from this epicenter,

    E.   In addition waves of motion travel out from this epicenter

Item 14.

    A.   often caused widespread destruction to an area.
    B.   often are caused widespread destruction to an area.
    C.   often causing widespread destruction to an area.
    D.   often are causing widespread destruction to an area.
    E.   often cause widespread destruction to an area.

Item 15.

    A.   With this likelihood for earthquakes to occur: it is essential that earthquake prediction systems are in place.
    B.   With this likelihood for earthquakes to occur; it is essential that earthquake prediction systems are in place.
    C.   With this likelihood for earthquakes to occur, it is essential that earthquake prediction systems are in place.
    D.   With this likelihood, for earthquakes to occur, it is essential that earthquake prediction systems are in place.
    E.   With this likelihood for earthquakes to occur it is essential that earthquake prediction systems are in place.

Item 16.

    A.   The purpose of earthquake prediction is to give advanced warning to the population,
    B   The purpose of earthquake prediction is give advanced warning to the population,
    C.   The purpose of earthquake prediction is giving advanced warning to the population,
    D.   The purpose of earthquake prediction giving advanced warning to the population,
    E.   The purpose of earthquake prediction is given advanced warning to the population,

Item 17.

    A.   with saving lives in the process.
    B.   now saving lives in the process.
    C.   at saving lives in the process.
    D.   in saving lives in the process.
    E.   thereby saving lives in the process.

Item 18.

    A.   Yet, this prediction systems need to be reliable in order to be of any practical use.
    B.   Yet, that prediction systems need to be reliable in order to be of any practical use.
    C.   Yet, these prediction systems need to be reliable in order to be of any practical use.
    D.   Yet, them prediction systems need to be reliable in order to be of any practical use.
    E.   Yet, there prediction systems need to be reliable in order to be of any practical use.

Item 19.

    A.   For this reason, scientists are currently attempting to conduct research
    B.   For this reason, scientists are currently attempt to conduct research
    C.   For this reason, scientists are currently attempting conduct research
    D.   For this reason, scientists are currently to attempting to conduct research
    E.   For this reason, scientists are currently attempting conducting research

Item 20.

    A.   on the probability of earthquakes along every of the 12 fault lines.
    B.   on the probability of earthquakes along each of the 12 fault lines.
    C.   on the probability of earthquakes all along of the 12 fault lines.
    D.   on the probability of earthquakes along of the 12 fault lines.
    E.   on the probability of earthquakes each and every of the 12 fault lines.

Item 21.

Which sentence, added to the end of the first paragraph, would emphasize the importance of the tectonic plates in causing earthquakes?

    A.   Therefore, the tectonic plates can be found both at land and at sea.
    B.   Both at land and at sea, the tectonic plates are present.
    C.   The tectonic plates, both at land and at sea, play a key role in producing earthquakes.
    D.   Of course, the tectonic plates therefore cause earthquakes, both at land and at sea.
    E.   Indeed, tectonic plates can be found problematically both at land at sea.

Item 22.

Imagine that the student has been assigned an essay to explain the reasons why current earthquake prediction systems are unreliable. Has the student achieved this purpose?

- A.   Yes, because the student states that earthquake systems need to be reliable.
- B.   Yes, because the student explains that scientists are conducting research on this issue.
- C.   Yes, because the student gives a great deal of background information about the problems caused by earthquakes.
- D.   No, because the student fails to give specific reasons why current prediction systems are unreliable.
- E.   No, because the student does not explain the focus of current earthquake research.

Writing Test 2

Abraham Lincoln

(*1*) In the fall of 1859, a discouraged man was sitting   (*2*) in his run-down law office in Springfield Illinois.   (*3*) He was fifty years old, and he had been a lawyer for twenty years, was earning on average 3,000 dollars a year.   (*4*) His tangible possessions and property consisted in 160 acres of farm land in Iowa   (*5*) and the house which he lived in Illinois.

(*6*) When his monetary resources were limited and he was in debt,   (*7*) this man can later go on to do great things for his country.   (*8*) His name was Abraham Lincoln.

(*9*) In 1859, some of Lincoln's associates had already begun to put down the idea (*10*) which he should run for president of the United States,   (*11*) a notion that he discounted in his usually self-deprecating manner.   (*12*) Yet, as time passed, Lincoln started to believe that his candidacy   (*13*) for United States President be possible.   (*14*) He began to write influential Republican Party leaders,   (*15*) including Norman Judd and Richard Oglesby, for its support.

(*16*) By 1860, Lincoln garnered more public support after having delivered public lectures and political speeches in various states.

(17) The Republican National Convention took place in Chicago, on May 16, 1860.

(18) William Seward, an popular outstandingly Republican leader, *(19)* predicted to win the nomination for the Republican Party. *(20)* Further, Lincoln won 354 of the 466 total votes.

(21) Thus: in November, 1860, Lincoln was elected as the President of the United States.

Writing Test 2

Item 1.

    A.   In the fall of 1859, a discouraged man was sitting
    B.   In the fall of 1859, a discouraged man is sitting
    C.   In the fall of 1859, a discouraged man sitting
    D.   In the fall of 1859, a discouraged man is seated
    E.   In the fall of 1859, a discouraged man seated

Item 2.

    A.   in his run-down law office in Springfield Illinois.
    B.   in his run-down law office in Springfield, Illinois.
    C.   in his run-down law office, in Springfield Illinois.
    D.   in his run-down law office, in Springfield, Illinois.
    E.   in his run-down, law office, in Springfield, Illinois.

Item 3.

    A.   He was fifty years old, and he had been a lawyer for twenty years, was earning on average 3,000 dollars a year.
    B.   He was fifty years old, and he had been a lawyer for twenty years, who earning on average 3,000 dollars a year.
    C.   He was fifty years old, and he had been a lawyer for twenty years, who is earning on average 3,000 dollars a year.
    D.   He was fifty years old, and he had been a lawyer for twenty years, earning on average 3,000 dollars a year.
    E.   He was fifty years old, and he had been a lawyer for twenty years, earned on average 3,000 dollars a year.

Item 4.

    A.   His tangible possessions and property consisted in 160 acres of farm land in Iowa
    B.   His tangible possessions and property consisted with 160 acres of farm land in Iowa
    C.   His tangible possessions and property consisted for 160 acres of farm land in Iowa
    D.   His tangible possessions and property consisted of 160 acres of farm land in Iowa
    E.   His tangible possessions and property consisted on 160 acres of farm land in Iowa

Item 5.

    A.   and the house which he lived in Illinois.
    B.   and the house in which he lived in Illinois.
    C.   and the house in that he lived in Illinois.
    D.   and the house in where he lived in Illinois.
    E.   and the house whose he lived in Illinois.

Item 6.

    A.   When his monetary resources were limited and he was in debt,
    B.   Although his monetary resources were limited and he was in debt,
    C.   Even his monetary resources were limited and he was in debt,
    D.   Thus his monetary resources were limited and he was in debt,
    E.   Hence his monetary resources were limited and he was in debt,

Item 7.

    A.   this man can later go on to do great things for his country.
    B.   this man could later go on to do great things for his country.
    C.   this man should later go on to do great things for his country.
    D.   this man would later go on to do great things for his country.
    E.   this man ought to later go on to do great things for his country.

Item 8.

    A.   His name was Abraham Lincoln.
    B.   His name is Abraham Lincoln.
    C.   His name Abraham Lincoln.
    D.   His name; Abraham Lincoln.
    E.   His name, Abraham Lincoln.

Item 9.

    A.   In 1859, some of Lincoln's associates had already begun to put down the idea
    B.   In 1859, some of Lincoln's associates had already begun to put against the idea
    C.   In 1859, some of Lincoln's associates had already begun to put forward the idea
    D.   In 1859, some of Lincoln's associates had already begun to put upon the idea
    E.   In 1859, some of Lincoln's associates had already begun to put with the idea

Item 10.

 A. which he should run for president of the United States,
 B. that he should run for president of the United States,
 C. whose he should run for president of the United States,
 D. whom he should run for president of the United States,
 E. who he should run for president of the United States,

Item 11.

 A. a notion that he discounted in his usually self-deprecating manner.
 B. a notion that he discounted in his usual self-deprecating manner.
 C. a notion that he discounted in his self, usual deprecating manner.
 D. a notion that he discounted in his self, usually deprecating manner.
 E. a notion that he discounted in his self-deprecating usually manner.

Item 12.

 A. Yet, as time passed, Lincoln started to believe that his candidacy
 B. Now, as time passed, Lincoln started to believe that his candidacy
 C. Thereupon, as time passed, Lincoln started to believe that his candidacy
 D. Because, as time passed, Lincoln started to believe that his candidacy
 E. Moreover, as time passed, Lincoln started to believe that his candidacy

Item 13.

 A. for United States President be possible.
 B. for United States President be possibly.
 C. for United States President might be possible.
 D. for United States President might be possibly.
 E. for United States President possible might be.

Item 14.

 A. He began to write influential Republican Party leaders,
 B. He began to write Republican influential Party leaders,
 C. He began to write Republican Party influential leaders,
 D. He began to write Republican Party leaders influential,
 E. He began influential to write Republican Party leaders,

Item 15.

A.   including Norman Judd and Richard Oglesby, for its support.
B.   including Norman Judd and Richard Oglesby, for it's support.
C.   including Norman Judd and Richard Oglesby, for his support.
D.   including Norman Judd and Richard Oglesby, for their support.
E.   including Norman Judd and Richard Oglesby, for them support.

Item 16.

A.   By 1860, Lincoln garnered more public support after having delivered public lectures and political speeches in various states.
B.   By 1860, Lincoln had garnered more public support after having delivered public lectures and political speeches in various states.
C.   By 1860, Lincoln has garnered more public support after having delivered public lectures and political speeches in various states.
D.   By 1860, Lincoln have garnered more public support after having delivered public lectures and political speeches in various states.
E.   By 1860, Lincoln having garnered more public support after having delivered public lectures and political speeches in various states.

Item 17.

A.   The Republican National Convention took place in Chicago, on May 16, 1860.
B.   The Republican National Convention took place in Chicago on May 16, 1860.
C.   The Republican, National Convention took place in Chicago, on May 16, 1860.
D.   The Republican, National Convention took place in Chicago on May 16, 1860.
E.   The Republican National Convention took place in Chicago on May 16 1860.

Item 18.

A.   William Seward, an popular outstandingly Republican leader,
B.   William Seward, an outstandingly popular Republican leader,
C.   William Seward, an popular Republican outstandingly leader,
D.   William Seward, an popular Republican leader outstandingly,
E.   William Seward, an popular Republican leader outstanding,

Item 19.

    A.   predicted to win the nomination for the Republican Party.
    B.   be predicted to win the nomination for the Republican Party.
    C.   to be predicted to win the nomination for the Republican Party.
    D.   was predicted to win the nomination for the Republican Party.
    E.   as predicted to win the nomination for the Republican Party.

Item 20.

    A.   Further, Lincoln won 354 of the 466 total votes.
    B.   Similarly, Lincoln won 354 of the 466 total votes.
    C.   Nevertheless, Lincoln won 354 of the 466 total votes.
    D.   Even though, Lincoln won 354 of the 466 total votes.
    E.   Despite, Lincoln won 354 of the 466 total votes.

Item 21.

    A.   Thus: in November, 1860, Lincoln was elected as the President of the United States.
    B.   Thus; in November, 1860, Lincoln was elected as the President of the United States.
    C.   Thus, in November 1860, Lincoln was elected as the President of the United States.
    D.   Thus, in November, 1860, Lincoln was elected as the President of the United States.
    E.   Thus, in November, 1860 Lincoln was elected as the President of the United States.

Item 22.

Suppose the student needs to explain why the Democratic Party lost the 1860 election. Which sentence, if added after the third sentence of the last paragraph, would achieve this purpose?

    A.   To win the election, the Democratic Party needed unity on the issue of slavery.
    B.   The Democratic Party ultimately could not unite on the issue of slavery.
    C.   The Democratic Party elected three different candidates on the issue of slavery.
    D.   The Democratic Party failed to win the election since, being divided on the issue of slavery, it elected three different candidates.
    E.   The Democratic Party could not win on the issue of slavery because it had three different candidates.

Writing Test 3

The Philosophy of Human Nature

(1) The study of the philosophy of human nature is often regarded as an investigation at the meaning of life. *(2)* This subject deals with four key problem areas: human choice, human thought, human personality, and the unity of the human being. *(3)* A consideration in these four problem areas *(4)* can include scientific also and artistic viewpoints on the nature of human life.

(5) The first problem area human choice, asks *(6)* whether human beings can really make decisions that can change their futures. *(7)* However, it investigates to what extent the individual's future is fixed *(8)* and pre-determined then cosmic forces outside the control of human beings.

(9) In the second problem area, human thought, epistemology is considering.

(10) Epistemology means the study of knowledge, it should not be confused with ontology, the study of being or existence.

(*11*) The third key issue, human personality, emphasized aspects of human life that are beyond mental processes. (*12*) They takes a look at emotional, spiritual, and communal elements. (*13*) Important, the study of the communal aspect focuses on community and communication, (*14*) instead on government or the philosophy of the state.

(*15*) Finally, the fourth problem, the unity of the human being, explores the first three areas more full (*16*) and asks if that there is any unifying basis for human choice, thought, and personality. (*17*) In other words, while the human is an inherently complex being, there must be a unity or wholeness which underlies these complications.

(*18*) The study of the philosophy of human nature can be enable an individual to contemplate more deeply vital human issues, (*19*) included an engagement with political, cultural, and social debates. (*20*) Not surprisingly, the works of Plato and Aristotle is generally regarded as the foundation for this subject.

Writing Test 3

Item 1.

    A.   The study of the philosophy of human nature is often regarded as an investigation at the meaning of life.

    B.   The study of the philosophy of human nature is often regarded as an investigation for the meaning of life.

    C.   The study of the philosophy of human nature is often regarded as an investigation about the meaning of life.

    D.   The study of the philosophy of human nature is often regarded as an investigation into the meaning of life.

    E.   The study of the philosophy of human nature is often regarded as an investigation within the meaning of life.

Item 2.

    A.   This subject deals with four key problem areas: human choice, human thought, human personality, and the unity of the human being.

    B.   This subject deals with four key problem areas, human choice, human thought, human personality, and the unity of the human being.

    C.   This subject deals with four key problem areas; human choice, human thought, human personality, and the unity of the human being.

    D.   This subject deals with four key problem areas human choice, human thought, human personality, and the unity of the human being.

    E.   This subject deals with four key problem areas. Human choice, human thought, human personality, and the unity of the human being.

Item 3.

    A.   A consideration in these four problem areas

    B.   A consideration with these four problem areas

    C.   A consideration for these four problem areas

    D.   A consideration against these four problem areas

    E.   A consideration of these four problem areas

Item 4.

    A.   can include scientific also and artistic viewpoints on the nature of human life.
    B.   can include scientific and artistic viewpoints also on the nature of human life.
    C.   can also include scientific and artistic viewpoints on the nature of human life.
    D.   can include scientific and artistic viewpoints on also the nature of human life.
    E.   can include scientific and artistic viewpoints on the nature also of human life.

Item 5.

    A.   The first problem area human choice, asks
    B.   The first problem area, human choice, asks
    C.   The first, problem area, human choice, asks
    D.   The first problem area human choice asks,
    E.   The first problem area human choice asks

Item 6.

    A.   whether human beings can really make decisions that can change their futures.
    B.   whether human beings can really make decisions that can change his futures.
    C.   whether human beings can really make decisions that can change its futures.
    D.   whether human beings can really make decisions that can change it's futures.
    E.   whether human beings can really make decisions that can change one's future.

Item 7.

    A.   However, it investigates to what extent the individual's future is fixed
    B.   Conversely, it investigates to what extent the individual's future is fixed
    C.   Negatively, it investigates to what extent the individual's future is fixed
    D.   Despite, it investigates to what extent the individual's future is fixed
    E.   In spite of it investigates to what extent the individual's future is fixed

Item 8.

    A.   and pre-determined then cosmic forces outside the control of human beings.
    B.   and pre-determined according cosmic forces outside the control of human beings.
    C.   and pre-determined by cosmic forces outside the control of human beings.
    D.   and pre-determined after cosmic forces outside the control of human beings.
    E.   and pre-determined since cosmic forces outside the control of human beings.

Item 9.

    A.   In the second problem area, human thought, epistemology is considering.

    B.   In the second problem area, human thought, epistemology considering.

    C.   In the second problem area, human thought, epistemology is considered.

    D.   In the second problem area, human thought, epistemology considered.

    E.   In the second problem area, human thought, epistemology being considered.

Item 10.

    A.   Epistemology means the study of knowledge, it should not be confused with ontology, the study of being or existence.

    B.   Epistemology means the study of knowledge: it should not be confused with ontology, the study of being or existence.

    C.   Epistemology means the study of knowledge; it should not be confused with ontology, the study of being or existence.

    D.   Epistemology means the study of knowledge, which it should not be confused with ontology, the study of being or existence.

    E.   Epistemology, means the study of knowledge, it should not be confused with ontology, the study of being or existence.

Item 11.

    A.   The third key issue, human personality, emphasized aspects of human life that are beyond mental processes.

    B.   The third key issue, human personality, had emphasized aspects of human life that are beyond mental processes.

    C.   The third key issue, human personality, is emphasizing aspects of human life that are beyond mental processes.

    D.   The third key issue, human personality, emphasizing aspects of human life that are beyond mental processes.

    E.   The third key issue, human personality, emphasizes aspects of human life that are beyond mental processes.

Item 12.

    A.   They takes a look at emotional, spiritual, and communal elements.
    B.   You takes a look at emotional, spiritual, and communal elements.
    C.   You take a look at emotional, spiritual, and communal elements.
    D.   One take a look at emotional, spiritual, and communal elements.
    E.   It takes a look at emotional, spiritual, and communal elements.

Item 13.

    A.   Important, the study of the communal aspect focuses on community and communication,
    B.   Importantly, the study of the communal aspect focuses on community and communication,
    C.   The importantly study of the communal aspect focuses on community and communication,
    D.   The study of the importantly communal aspect focuses on community and communication,
    E.   The study of the communal importantly aspect focuses on community and communication,

Item 14.

    A.   instead on government or the philosophy of the state.
    B.   rather on government or the philosophy of the state.
    C.   rather than on government or the philosophy of the state.
    D.   besides on government or the philosophy of the state.
    E.   beside that on government or the philosophy of the state.

Item 15.

    A.   Finally, the fourth problem, the unity of the human being, explores the first three areas more full
    B.   Finally, the fourth problem, the unity of the human being, explores the first three areas more fully
    C.   Finally, the fourth problem, the unity of the human being, explores the first more fully three areas
    D.   Finally, the fourth problem, the unity of the human being, explores the first more full three areas
    E.   Finally, the fourth problem, the unity of the human being, explores the more fully first three areas

Item 16.

    A.   and asks if that there is any unifying basis for human choice, thought, and personality.

    B.   and asks if is any unifying basis for human choice, thought, and personality.

    C.   and asks whether there is any unifying basis for human choice, thought, and personality.

    D.   and asks whether is there any unifying basis for human choice, thought, and personality.

    E.   and asks is whether there any unifying basis for human choice, thought, and personality.

Item 17.

    A.   In other words, while the human is an inherently complex being, there must be a unity or wholeness which underlies these complications.

    B.   In other words, while the human is an inherently complex being, there must be a unity or wholeness which underlied these complications.

    C.   In other words, while the human is an inherently complex being, there must be a unity or wholeness that underlying these complications.

    D.   In other words, while the human is an inherently complex being, there must be a unity or wholeness whose underlying these complications.

    E.   In other words, while the human is an inherently complex being, there must be a unity or wholeness whose underlies these complications.

Item 18.

    A.   The study of the philosophy of human nature can be enable an individual to contemplate more deeply vital human issues,

    B.   The study of the philosophy of human nature can be enabled an individual to contemplate more deeply vital human issues,

    C.   The study of the philosophy of human nature should be enable an individual to contemplate more deeply vital human issues,

    D.   The study of the philosophy of human nature should enable an individual to contemplate more deeply vital human issues,

    E.   The study of the philosophy of human nature should be enabled an individual to contemplate more deeply vital human issues,

Item 19.

    A.   included an engagement with political, cultural, and social debates.
    B.   including an engagement with political, cultural, and social debates.
    C.   inclusive an engagement with political, cultural, and social debates.
    D.   inclusion an engagement with political, cultural, and social debates.
    E.   inclusion of an engagement with political, cultural, and social debates.

Item 20.

    A.   Not surprisingly, the works of Plato and Aristotle is generally regarded as the foundation for this subject.
    B.   Not surprisingly, the works of Plato and Aristotle are generally regarded as the foundation for this subject.
    C.   Not surprisingly, the works of Plato and Aristotle is regarded generally as the foundation for this subject.
    D.   Not surprisingly, the works of Plato and Aristotle were generally regarded as the foundation for this subject.
    E.   Not surprisingly, the works of Plato and Aristotle were regarded generally as the foundation for this subject.

Item 21.

Imagine that the student wanted to add a sentence to the second paragraph emphasizing the reasons for the importance of human choice. Which of the following sentences accomplishes this?

    A.   A sense of control over one's life is also extremely important.
    B.   Feeling in control of one's life is important for individuals who believe in destiny.
    C.   Feelings of individual control support the belief in chance, fate, and destiny.
    D.   A sense of control over one's life can enable an individual to make empowering decisions about his or her future.
    E.   Superstition plays a role in the lives of many who lack control over their lives.

Item 22.

If the student were to eliminate the last paragraph of the essay, the essay would lack

    A.   a comparison of ancient and modern philosophy.
    B.   an explanation of the outcome of the study of philosophy.
    C.   an insight into the attitudes of some of the world's most important philosophers.
    D.   the inference that philosophy is an abstruse subject.
    E.   the recommendation of which books a student of philosophy should read.

Writing Test 4

Organic Food

(*1*) <u>Organic farming and organic produce even though create many positive outcomes</u>

<u>for the environment,</u>   (*2*) <u>mostly mainstream American consumers have reservations about</u>

<u>organic food.</u>

(*3*) <u>The first drawback that consumers perceive is of course, cost.</u>   (*4*) <u>Organic food</u>

<u>often costs 50 to 100 percent much more than food produced using traditional farming</u>

<u>methods.</u>   (*5*) <u>Consumers with higher income levels probably afforded this,</u>   (*6*) <u>but many</u>

<u>people simple do not believe than the potential health and environmental benefits are worth the</u>

<u>expense.</u>

(*7*) <u>There also concerns about the safety of organic food.</u>   (*8*) <u>Organic produce often</u>

<u>grown using cow manure.</u>   (*9*) <u>Take the case of windfall apples, which are apples that fall off</u>

<u>the tree.</u>   (*10*) <u>These apples can be contaminated by the cow manure, and if not washes</u>

<u>properly, this can lead to serious food poisoning or even death.</u>   (*11*) <u>This contamination</u>

<u>occurs because manure contains a very insecure bacteria, known as e-coli.</u>

(12) Last but not least, and strangely enough, some people are reluctant to purchase organic food because he thinks it spoils too quickly. *(13)* Food preservative's are not natural ingredients in food, but they do, in many cases, substantially prolong the life of food.

(14) This long-life in the minds makes the non-organic food a better value of many consumers.

(15) So, it may be quite some time before the purchase of organic food became the norm in American households.

Writing Test 4

Item 1.

    A.   Organic farming and organic produce even though create many positive outcomes for the environment,

    B.   Organic farming and organic produce even though creating many positive outcomes for the environment,

    C.   Even though organic farming and organic produce create many positive outcomes for the environment,

    D.   Organic farming and organic produce create even though many positive outcomes for the environment,

    E.   Organic farming and organic produce create many positive outcomes even though for the environment,

Item 2.

    A.   mostly mainstream American consumers have reservations about organic food.

    B.   most mainstream American consumers have reservations about organic food.

    C.   mainstream mostly American consumers have reservations about organic food.

    D.   mainstream most American consumers have reservations about organic food.

    E.   mainstream American most consumers have reservations about organic food.

Item 3.

    A.   The first drawback that consumers perceive is of course, cost.

    B.   The first drawback, that consumers perceive is of course, cost.

    C.   The first drawback, that consumers perceive is of course cost.

    D.   The first drawback that consumers perceive is, of course, cost.

    E.   The first, drawback that consumers perceive is of course cost.

Item 4.

    A.   Organic food often costs 50 to 100 percent much more than food produced using traditional farming methods.

    B.   Organic food often costs 50 to 100 percent much than food produced using traditional farming methods.

    C.   Organic food often costs 50 to 100 percent than food produced using traditional farming methods.

    D.   Organic food often costs 50 to 100 percent most than food produced using traditional farming methods.

E.   Organic food often costs 50 to 100 percent more than food produced using traditional farming methods.

Item 5.

A.   Consumers with higher income levels probably afforded this,
B.   Consumers with higher income levels can probably afforded this,
C.   Consumers with higher income levels are probable to afford this,
D.   Consumers with higher income levels are probably afforded this,
E.   Consumers with higher income levels can probably afford this,

Item 6.

A.   but many people simple do not believe than the potential health and environmental benefits are worth the expense.
B.   but many people simple do not believe that the potential health and environmental benefits are worth the expense.
C.   but many people simple do not believe, which the potential health and environmental benefits are worth the expense.
D.   but many people simple do not believe which the potential health and environmental benefits are worth the expense.
E.   but many people simply do not believe that the potential health and environmental benefits are worth the expense.

Item 7.

A.   There also concerns about the safety of organic food.
B.   There is also concerns about the safety of organic food.
C.   There are also concerns about the safety of organic food.
D.   Concerning about the safety of organic food.
E.   Concerning the safety of organic food.

Item 8.

A.   Organic produce often grown using cow manure.
B.   Organic produce is often grown using cow manure.
C.   Organic produce often grown is using cow manure.
D.   Organic produce grown often using cow manure.
E.   Organic produce grown is using often cow manure.

Item 9.

    A.   Take the case of windfall apples, which are apples that fall off the tree.
    B.   Take the case of windfall apples, that are apples that fall off the tree.
    C.   Take the case of windfall apples, are apples that fall off the tree.
    D.   Take the case of windfall apples, whose apples that fall off the tree.
    E.   Take the case of windfall apples, in which apples that fall off the tree.

Item 10.

    A.   These apples can be contaminated by the cow manure, and if not washes properly, this can lead to serious food poisoning or even death.
    B.   These apples can be contaminated by the cow manure, and if not washed properly, this can lead to serious food poisoning or even death.
    C.   These apples can be contaminated by the cow manure, and if not being washed properly, this can lead to serious food poisoning or even death.
    D.   These apples can be contaminated by the cow manure, and if do not washed properly, this can lead to serious food poisoning or even death.
    E.   These apples can be contaminated by the cow manure, and if not will be washed properly, this can lead to serious food poisoning or even death.

Item 11.

    A.   This contamination occurs because manure contains a very insecure bacteria, known as e-coli.
    B.   This contamination occurs because manure contains a very harming bacteria, known as e-coli.
    C.   This contamination occurs because manure contains a very dangerous bacteria, known as e-coli.
    D.   This contamination occurs because manure contains a very defenseless bacteria, known as e-coli.
    E.   This contamination occurs because manure contains a very vulnerable bacteria, known as e-coli.

Item 12.

   A. Last but not least, and strangely enough, some people are reluctant to purchase organic food because he thinks it spoils too quickly.
   B. Last but not least, and strangely enough, some people are reluctant to purchase organic food because they think it spoils too quickly.
   C. Last but not least, and strangely enough, some people are reluctant to purchase organic food because one thinks it spoils too quickly.
   D. Last but not least, and strangely enough, some people are reluctant to purchase organic food because you think it spoils too quickly.
   E. Last but not least, and strangely enough, some people are reluctant to purchase organic food because it thinks it spoils too quickly.

Item 13.

   A. Food preservative's are not natural ingredients in food, but they do, in many cases, substantially prolong the life of food.
   B. Food preservatives' are not natural ingredients in food, but they do, in many cases, substantially prolong the life of food.
   C. Food preservatives are not natural ingredients in food, but they do, in many cases, substantially prolong the life of food.
   D. Food's preservatives are not natural ingredients in food, but they do, in many cases, substantially prolong the life of food.
   E. Foods' preservatives are not natural ingredients in food, but they do, in many cases, substantially prolong the life of food.

Item 14.

   A. This long-life in the minds makes the non-organic food a better value of many consumers.
   B. This long-life makes the non-organic food in the minds a better value of many consumers.
   C. This long-life makes in the minds the non-organic food a better value of many consumers.
   D. In the minds, this long-life makes the non-organic food a better value in the minds of many consumers.
   E. This long-life makes the non-organic food a better value in the minds of many consumers.

Item 15.

A. So, it may be quite some time before the purchase of organic food became the norm in American households.
B. So, it may be quite some time before the purchase of organic food becomes the norm in American households.
C. So, it may be quite some time before the purchase of organic food become the norm in American households.
D. So, it may be quite some time before the purchase of organic food is becoming the norm in American households.
E. So, it may be quite some time before the purchase of organic food had become the norm in American households.

Item 16.

Suppose the student wants to add a sentence at the end of the last paragraph to make a prediction about future purchase of organic food by the American public. Which of the following sentences would achieve that purpose?

A. But the main reason why members of the public refuse to purchase organic food will be because of its cost.
B. Normally in the future the production of organic food is bound to decline.
C. Looking ahead, organic produce may become a better value for American consumers.
D. If prices were reduced, organic food sales to the public would increase in the future.
E. Without increased public demand, the organic food industry will not improve in its profitability.

Writing Test 5

Antarctica

(*1*) <u>Antarctica is a mysterious and trustworthy continent</u>   (*2*) <u>one which is often</u>

<u>forgotten by virtue of its geographical location.</u>   (*3*) <u>Now that the Antarctic is remote and</u>

<u>desolate.</u>   (*4*) <u>Nevertheless, an understanding of the organisms that inhabit this continent was</u>

<u>critical</u>   (*5*) <u>to our comprehension of the world as a global community.</u>   (*6*) <u>For this reason, the</u>

<u>southernmost continent has the source of a great deal of scientific investigation.</u>

(*7*) <u>Many notable recent research has come from America and Great Britain.</u>   (*8*) <u>The</u>

<u>British Antarctic Survey, sponsored with the Natural Environment Research Council of the</u>

<u>United Kingdom,</u>   (*9*) <u>and the United States Antarctic Resource Center, a collaborate of the</u>

<u>United States Geological Survey Mapping Division and the National Science Foundation,</u>

(*10*) <u>are forerunners in the burgeoning currently field of research in this area.</u>

(*11*) <u>This corpus of research has resulted in an abundance of factual data on the</u>

<u>Antarctic.</u>   (*12*) <u>For example, one now know that more than ninety nine percent of the land is</u>

<u>completely covered by snow and ice,</u>   (*13*) <u>which making Antarctica the coldest continent on</u>

the planet. *(14)* This inhospitable climate, has not surprisingly, brought about the adaptation

(15) of a plethora of plants and biological organisms on the continent present. *(16)* An

investigation for the sedimentary geological formations provides testimony to the process of

adaptation. *(17)* Ancient sediment's recovered from the bottom of Antarctic lakes, *(18)*

bacteria as well as discovered in ice, *(19)* has reveal the history of climate change over the

past 10,000 years.

Item 1.

    A.   Antarctica is a mysterious and trustworthy continent
    B.   Antarctica is a mysterious and resilient continent
    C.   Antarctica is a mysterious and respectable continent
    D.   Antarctica is a mysterious and characteristic continent
    E.   Antarctica is a mysterious and shy continent

Item 2.

    A.   one which is often forgotten by virtue of its geographical location.
    B.   one whose often forgotten by virtue of its geographical location.
    C.   that is often forgotten by virtue of its geographical location.
    D.   this is often forgotten by virtue of its geographical location.
    E.   those are often forgotten by virtue of its geographical location.

Item 3.

    A.   Now that the Antarctic is remote and desolate.
    B.   Always, the Antarctic is remote and desolate.
    C.   Since the Antarctic is remote and desolate.
    D.   Indeed, the Antarctic is remote and desolate.
    E.   On the other hand, the Antarctic is remote and desolate.

Item 4.

    A.   Nevertheless, an understanding of the organisms that inhabit this continent was critical
    B.   Nevertheless, an understanding of the organisms that inhabit this continent were critical
    C.   Nevertheless, an understanding of the organisms that inhabit this continent is critical
    D.   Nevertheless, an understanding of the organisms that inhabit this continent are critical
    E.   Nevertheless, an understanding of the organisms that inhabit this continent are being critical

Item 5.

    A.   to our comprehension of the world as a global community.
    B.   to our comprehension at the world as a global community.
    C.   to our comprehension in the world as a global community.
    D.   to our comprehension about the world as a global community.
    E.   to our comprehension for the world as a global community.

Item 6.

    A.   For this reason, the southernmost continent has the source of a great deal of scientific investigation.
    B.   For this reason, the southernmost continent has been the source of a great deal of scientific investigation.
    C.   For this reason, the southernmost continent was the source of a great deal of scientific investigation.
    D.   For this reason, the southernmost continent has to be the source of a great deal of scientific investigation.
    E.   For this reason, the southernmost continent had the source of a great deal of scientific investigation.

Item 7.

    A.   Many notable recent research has come from America and Great Britain.
    B.   Much notable recent research has come from America and Great Britain.
    C.   More notable recent research has come from America and Great Britain.
    D.   More than notable recent research has come from America and Great Britain.
    E.   As much as notable recent research has come from America and Great Britain.

Item 8.

    A.   The British Antarctic Survey, sponsored with the Natural Environment Research Council of the United Kingdom,
    B.   The British Antarctic Survey, sponsored by the Natural Environment Research Council of the United Kingdom,
    C.   The British Antarctic Survey, sponsored against the Natural Environment Research Council of the United Kingdom,
    D.   The British Antarctic Survey, sponsored from the Natural Environment Research Council of the United Kingdom,
    E.   The British Antarctic Survey, sponsored upon the Natural Environment Research Council of the United Kingdom,

Item 9.

    A.   and the United States Antarctic Resource Center, a collaborate of the United States Geological Survey Mapping Division and the National Science Foundation,

    B.   And the United States Antarctic Resource Center, a collaborative of the United States Geological Survey Mapping Division and the National Science Foundation,

    C.   and the United States Antarctic Resource Center, a collaboratively of the United States Geological Survey Mapping Division and the National Science Foundation,

    D.   and the United States Antarctic Resource Center, a collaboration of the United States Geological Survey Mapping Division and the National Science Foundation,

    E.   and the United States Antarctic Resource Center, a collaborator of the United States Geological Survey Mapping Division and the National Science Foundation,

Item 10.

    A.   are forerunners in the burgeoning currently field of research in this area.

    B.   are forerunners in the burgeoning field of currently research in this area.

    C.   are currently forerunners in the burgeoning field of research in this area.

    D.   are forerunners in the burgeoning field of research in currently this area.

    E.   are forerunners in the burgeoning field of research in this currently area.

Item 11.

    A.   This corpus of research has resulted in an abundance of factual data on the Antarctic.

    B.   This corpus of research was resulted in an abundance of factual data on the Antarctic.

    C.   This corpus of research has been resulted in an abundance of factual data on the Antarctic.

    D.   This corpus of research was resulting in an abundance of factual data on the Antarctic.

    E.   This corpus of research resulting in an abundance of factual data on the Antarctic.

Item 12.

    A.   For example, one now know that more than ninety nine percent of the land is completely covered by snow and ice,

    B.   For example, we now know that more than ninety nine percent of the land is completely covered by snow and ice,

    C.   For example, they now knows that more than ninety nine percent of the land is completely covered by snow and ice,

    D.   For example, the community now know that more than ninety nine percent of the land is completely covered by snow and ice,

    E.   For example, the research now know that more than ninety nine percent of the land is completely covered by snow and ice,

Item 13.

    A.   which making Antarctica the coldest continent on the planet.

    B.   which is making Antarctica the coldest continent on the planet.

    C.   making Antarctica the coldest continent on the planet.

    D.   has made Antarctica the coldest continent on the planet.

    E.   that made Antarctica the coldest continent on the planet.

Item 14.

    A.   This inhospitable climate, has not surprisingly, brought about the adaptation

    B.   This inhospitable climate has, not surprisingly, brought about the adaptation

    C.   This inhospitable climate has, not surprisingly; brought about the adaptation

    D.   This inhospitable climate has not surprisingly: brought about the adaptation

    E.   This inhospitable climate has not surprisingly, brought about the adaptation

Item 15.

    A.   of a plethora of plants and biological organisms on the continent present.

    B.   of a plethora of plants and biological organisms present on the continent.

    C.   of a plethora on the continent of plants and biological organisms present.

    D.   of a plethora of plants on the continent and biological organisms present.

    E.   of a plethora of plants and on the continent biological organisms present.

Item 16.

    A.   An investigation for the sedimentary geological formations provides testimony to the process of adaptation.

    B.   An investigation within the sedimentary geological formations provides testimony to the process of adaptation.

    C.   An investigation at the sedimentary geological formations provides testimony to the process of adaptation.

    D.   An investigation about the sedimentary geological formations provides testimony to the process of adaptation.

    E.   An investigation into the sedimentary geological formations provides testimony to the process of adaptation.

Item 17.

    A.   Ancient sediment's recovered from the bottom of Antarctic lakes,

    B.   Ancient sediments' recovered from the bottom of Antarctic lakes,

    C.   Ancient sediments recovered from the bottom of Antarctic lakes,

    D.   Ancient's sediment recovered from the bottom of Antarctic lakes,

    E.   Ancient's sediments recovered from the bottom of Antarctic lakes,

Item 18.

    A.   bacteria as well as discovered in ice,

    B.   as well as bacteria discovered in ice,

    C.   bacteria discovered as well as in ice,

    D.   bacteria discovered in as well as ice,

    E.   bacteria discovered in ice as well,

Item 19.

    A.   has reveal the history of climate change over the past 10,000 years.

    B.   has revealed the history of climate change over the past 10,000 years.

    C.   have reveal the history of climate change over the past 10,000 years.

    D.   have revealed the history of climate change over the past 10,000 years.

    E.   have been revealed the history of climate change over the past 10,000 years.

Item 20.

If the student were to add a paragraph at the end of the essay explaining that the reliability of the research on Antarctica has been disputed, the essay would lose:

A.   its academic tone.
B.   its clarity and focus.
C.   the sense that this topic of current interest.
D.   its emphasis on the inhospitality of the Antarctic climate.
E.   the sense of importance it places on the scientific evidence.

Writing Test 6

Population Age-Sex Structure

    (1) <u>The major significant characteristic of any population is its age-sex structure,</u> *(2)*

<u>defining as the proportion of people of each gender in each different age group.</u> *(3)* <u>The sex-</u>

<u>age structure determines the potential for reproduction,</u> *(4)* <u>and for example population</u>

<u>growth,</u> *(5)* <u>based on the balance of males and females of child-bearing age inside a</u>

<u>population.</u> *(6)* <u>Thus, the age-sex structure was social policy implications.</u> *(7)* <u>For instance, a</u>

<u>population with a high proportion of citizens elderly</u> *(8)* <u>needs to consider its governmental-</u>

<u>funded pension schemes and health care systems carefully.</u> *(9)* <u>As follows: a demographic</u>

<u>with a greater percentage of young children should ensure</u> *(10)* <u>which its educational funding</u>

<u>and child welfare policies are implemented efficaciously.</u> *(11)* <u>Accordingly, as the</u>

<u>composition of a population changes against time,</u> *(12)* <u>the government may need to restate its</u>

<u>funding priorities.</u>

    (13) <u>For it is possible that a population may have low birth rates</u> *(14)* <u>resulting an</u>

<u>imbalance in the age-sex structure.</u> *(15)* <u>Low birth rate's might also be attributable to</u>

governmental policy that attempts to control the population.   *(16)* Policies are one example of

that restrict the number of children a family can have this outcome.   *(17)* Other possible reason

for these types of demographic changes might be unnaturally high death rates,   *(18)* such like

in the case of a disease epidemic or natural disaster.   *(19)* Finally, migration is another factor

(20) in demographic attrition, because in any population, a certain amount of people, may

decide to emigrate, or move to a different country.

Writing Test 6

Item 1.

    A.   The major significant characteristic of any population is its age-sex structure,

    B.   The majorly significant characteristic of any population is its age-sex structure,

    C.   The most significantly characteristic of any population is its age-sex structure,

    D.   The most significant characteristic of any population is its age-sex structure,

    E.   The more significant characteristic of any population is its age-sex structure,

Item 2.

    A.   defining as the proportion of people of each gender in each different age group.

    B.   defined as the proportion of people of each gender in each different age group.

    C.   which defining as the proportion of people of each gender in each different age group.

    D.   which defined as the proportion of people of each gender in each different age group.

    E.   as defined as the proportion of people of each gender in each different age group.

Item 3.

    A.   The sex-age structure determines the potential for reproduction,

    B.   The sex-age structure determined the potential for reproduction,

    C.   The sex-age structure has determined the potential for reproduction,

    D.   The sex-age structure had determined the potential for reproduction,

    E.   The sex-age structure was determined the potential for reproduction,

Item 4.

    A.   and for example population growth,

    B.   and so that population growth,

    C.   and with regard to population growth,

    D.   and it follows that population growth,

    E.   and as a consequence population growth,

Item 5.

    A.   based on the balance of males and females of child-bearing age inside a population.
    B.   based on the balance of males and females of child-bearing age within a population.
    C.   based on the balance of males and females of child-bearing age containing a population.
    D.   based on the balance of males and females of child-bearing age consisting a population.
    E.   based on the balance of males and females of child-bearing age attributing a population.

Item 6.

    A.   Thus, the age-sex structure was social policy implications.
    B.   Thus, the age-sex structure is social policy implications.
    C.   Thus, the age-sex structure has social policy implications.
    D.   Thus, the age-sex structure had social policy implications.
    E.   Thus, the age-sex structure does social policy implications.

Item 7.

    A.   For instance, a population with a high proportion of citizens elderly
    B.   For instance, a population with an elderly high proportion of citizens
    C.   For instance, a population with a high proportion elderly of citizens
    D.   For instance, a population with a high proportion of elderly citizens
    E.   For instance, a population with a high elderly proportion of citizens

Item 8.

    A.   needs to consider its governmental-funded pension schemes and health care systems carefully.
    B.   needs to consider its governmentally-funded pension schemes and health care systems carefully.
    C.   needs to consider its funded-governmental pension schemes and health care systems carefully.
    D.   needs to consider its funded-governmentally pension schemes and health care systems carefully.
    E.   needs to consider its funded governmentally-pension schemes and health care systems carefully.

Item 9.

    A.   As follows: a demographic with a greater percentage of young children should ensure

    B.   Just as a demographic with a greater percentage of young children should ensure

    C.   Conversely, a demographic with a greater percentage of young children should ensure

    D.   Despite, a demographic with a greater percentage of young children should ensure

    E.   Unless a demographic with a greater percentage of young children should ensure

Item 10.

    A.   which its educational funding and child welfare policies are implemented efficaciously.

    B.   that its educational funding and child welfare policies are implemented efficaciously.

    C.   which it's educational funding and child welfare policies are implemented efficaciously.

    D.   that it's educational funding and child welfare policies are implemented efficaciously.

    E.   hence its educational funding and child welfare policies are implemented efficaciously.

Item 11.

    A.   Accordingly, as the composition of a population changes against time,

    B.   Accordingly, as the composition of a population changes for time,

    C.   Accordingly, as the composition of a population changes over time,

    D.   Accordingly, as the composition of a population changes past time,

    E.   Accordingly, as the composition of a population changes as time,

Item 12.

    A.   the government may need to restate its funding priorities.
    B.   the government may need to re-evaluate its funding priorities.
    C.   the government may need to recuperate its funding priorities.
    D.   the government may need to cooperate its funding priorities.
    E.   the government may need to instigate its funding priorities.

Item 13.

    A.   For it is possible that a population may have low birth rates
    B.   For this possible that a population may have low birth rates
    C.   This is possible that a population may have low birth rates
    D.   It is possible that a population may have low birth rates
    E.   That is possible that a population may have low birth rates

Item 14.

    A.   resulting an imbalance in the age-sex structure.
    B.   because an imbalance in the age-sex structure.
    C.   due to an imbalance in the age-sex structure.
    D.   since an imbalance in the age-sex structure.
    E.   in order to imbalance in the age-sex structure.

Item 15.

    A.   Low birth rate's might also be attributable to governmental policy that attempts to control the population.
    B.   Low birth's rates might also be attributable to governmental policy that attempts to control the population.
    C.   Low births' rates might also be attributable to governmental policy that attempts to control the population.
    D.   Low birth rates' might also be attributable to governmental policy that attempts to control the population.
    E.   Low birth rates might also be attributable to governmental policy that attempts to control the population.

Item 16.

    A.   Policies are one example of that restrict the number of children a family can have this outcome.

    B.   Policies that restrict are one example of the number of children a family can have this outcome.

    C.   Policies that restrict the number of children a family can have this outcome are one example.

    D.   Policies that restrict the number of children a family can have are one example of this outcome.

    E.   Policies that restrict the number of children a family are one example of this outcome can have.

Item 17.

    A.   Other possible reason for these types of demographic changes might be unnaturally high death rates,

    B.   Others possible reason for these types of demographic changes might be unnaturally high death rates,

    C.   Another possible reason for these types of demographic changes might be unnaturally high death rates,

    D.   Anothers possible reason for these types of demographic changes might be unnaturally high death rates,

    E.   Another possible reasons for these types of demographic changes might be unnaturally high death rates,

Item 18.

    A.   such like in the case of a disease epidemic or natural disaster.

    B.   such as in the case of a disease epidemic or natural disaster.

    C.   as such as in the case of a disease epidemic or natural disaster.

    D.   as much as in the case of a disease epidemic or natural disaster.

    E.   as much like as in the case of a disease epidemic or natural disaster.

Item 19.

    A.   Finally, migration is another factor
    B.   Final migration is another factor
    C.   Final, migration is another factor
    D.   To end, migration is another factor
    E.   Conclusively, migration is another factor

Item 20.

    A.   in demographic attrition, because in any population, a certain amount of people, may decide to emigrate, or move to a different country.
    B.   in demographic attrition because in any population a certain amount of people may decide to emigrate, or move to a different country.
    C.   in demographic attrition, because in any population, a certain amount of people may decide to emigrate or move to a different country.
    D.   in demographic attrition because in any population, a certain amount of people may decide to emigrate, or move to a different country.
    E.   in demographic attrition because in any population a certain amount of people may decide to emigrate or move to a different country.

Item 21.

Suppose that the student was asked to write an essay, the purpose of which was to explain how the government could rectify current deficiencies in the age-sex structure. Has the student achieved this purpose?

    A.   Yes, because the student talks about the government's reassessment of funding priorities.
    B.   Yes, because the student describes the social policy implication of the age-sex structure.
    C.   Yes, because the student explains the effect of governmental policy on low birth rates.
    D.   No, because the student fails to provide sufficient examples of the how governmental policy needs to adapt to population changes over time.
    E.   No, because the student does not enumerate specific solutions that the government could attempt.

Writing Test 7

The Pilgrims

(*1*) A group of English separatists known as the pilgrims first left England to live in Amsterdam, in 1608. (*2*) After spending a few years in their new city, apart from this, many members of the group (*3*) felt whose they did not have enough independence. (*4*) Hence, in 1617, the pilgrims decided to leave Amsterdam immigrating to America.

(*5*) More of these separatists were poor farmers (*6*) whom did not have much education or social status, and, not surprisingly, (*7*) the group had many financial problems that prevented them for beginning their journey. (*8*) Thereby their inability to finance themselves caused many disputes and disagreements, (*9*) the pilgrims finally managing to obtain financing (*10*) from a well-known and considerable London businessman named Thomas Weston.

(*11*) Having secured Weston's monetary support, the group returned to England to pick up some additional passengers, (*12*) and it boarded a large ship called the *Mayflower* on September 16, 1620. (*13*) After 65 days at sea, the pilgrim's reached America. (*14*) Plymouth a town about 35 miles southeast of Boston in the New England state of Massachusetts *(15)*

was established by the pilgrims in December 21, 1620.   *(16)* Even though the early days of this

new lives were filled with hope and promise,   *(17)* the harsh winter proved being too much for

some of the settlers.   *(18)* Near half of the pilgrims died during that first winter,   *(19)* but those

who lived go on to work hard and prosper.

Writing Test 7

Item 1.

    A.   A group of English separatists known as the pilgrims first left England to live in Amsterdam, in 1608.

    B.   A group of English separatists known as the pilgrims first left England to live, in Amsterdam, in 1608.

    C.   A group of English separatists known as the pilgrims first left England to live in Amsterdam in 1608.

    D.   A group of English separatists known as the pilgrims, first left England to live in Amsterdam, in 1608.

    E.   A group of English separatists known as the pilgrims, first left England to live, in Amsterdam in 1608.

Item 2.

    A.   After spending a few years in their new city, apart from this, many members of the group

    B.   After spending a few years in their new city, in this case, many members of the group

    C.   After spending a few years in their new city, namely, many members of the group

    D.   After spending a few years in their new city, however, many members of the group

    E.   After spending a few years in their new city, otherwise, many members of the group

Item 3.

    A.   felt whose they did not have enough independence.

    B.   felt whom they did not have enough independence.

    C.   felt which they did not have enough independence.

    D.   felt that they did not have enough independence.

    E.   felt in that they did not have enough independence.

Item 4.

    A.   Hence, in 1617, the pilgrims decided to leave Amsterdam immigrating to America.
    B.   Hence, in 1617, the pilgrims decided to leave Amsterdam to immigrate to America.
    C.   Hence, in 1617, the pilgrims decided to leave Amsterdam emigrating to America.
    D.   Hence, in 1617, the pilgrims decided to leave Amsterdam to emigrate to America.
    E.   Hence, in 1617, the pilgrims decided to leave Amsterdam for migrating to America.

Item 5.

    A.   More of these separatists were poor farmers
    B.   Much of these separatists were poor farmers
    C.   Many of these separatists were poor farmers
    D.   Many more of these separatists were poor farmers
    E.   The most of these separatists were poor farmers

Item 6.

    A.   whom did not have much education or social status, and, not surprisingly,
    B.   of whom did not have much education or social status, and, not surprisingly,
    C.   whose did not have much education or social status, and, not surprisingly,
    D.   which did not have much education or social status, and, not surprisingly,
    E.   who did not have much education or social status, and, not surprisingly,

Item 7.

    A.   the group had many financial problems that prevented them for beginning their journey.
    B.   the group had many financial problems that prevented them to beginning their journey.
    C.   the group had many financial problems that prevented them from beginning their journey.
    D.   the group had many financial problems that prevented them against beginning their journey.
    E.   the group had many financial problems that prevented them with beginning their journey.

Item 8.

- A.   Thereby their inability to finance themselves caused many disputes and disagreements,
- B.   Although their inability to finance themselves caused many disputes and disagreements,
- C.   Nevertheless their inability to finance themselves caused many disputes and disagreements,
- D.   Despite their inability to finance themselves caused many disputes and disagreements,
- E.   In spite of their inability to finance themselves caused many disputes and disagreements,

Item 9.

- A.   the pilgrims finally managing to obtain financing
- B.   the pilgrims finally managed obtaining financing
- C.   the pilgrims finally were managed obtaining financing
- D.   the pilgrims finally were managed to obtain financing
- E.   the pilgrims finally managed to obtain financing

Item 10.

- A.   from a well-known and considerable London businessman named Thomas Weston.
- B.   From a well-known and affluent London businessman named Thomas Weston.
- C.   from a well-known and unfortunate London businessman named Thomas Weston.
- D.   from a well-known and adamant London businessman named Thomas Weston.
- E.   from a well-known and insistent London businessman named Thomas Weston.

Item 11.

- A.   Having secured Weston's monetary support, the group returned to England to pick up some additional passengers,
- B.   To have secured Weston's monetary support, the group returned to England to pick up some additional passengers,
- C.   They have secured Weston's monetary support, the group returned to England to pick up some additional passengers,
- D.   When they have secured Weston's monetary support, the group returned to England to pick up some additional passengers,
- E.   If having secured Weston's monetary support, the group returned to England to pick up some additional passengers,

Item 12.

A.   and it boarded a large ship called the Mayflower on September 16, 1620.
B.   and he or she boarded a large ship called the Mayflower on September 16, 1620.
C.   and one boarded a large ship called the Mayflower on September 16, 1620.
D.   and they boarded a large ship called the Mayflower on September 16, 1620.
E.   and those boarded a large ship called the Mayflower on September 16, 1620.

Item 13.

A.   After 65 days at sea, the pilgrim's reached America.
B.   After 65 days at sea, the pilgrims' reached America.
C.   After 65 days at sea, the pilgrims reached America.
D.   After 65 days at sea, pilgrim's reached America.
E.   After 65 days at sea, pilgrims' reached America.

Item 14.

A.   Plymouth a town about 35 miles southeast of Boston in the New England state of Massachusetts
B.   Plymouth, a town about 35 miles southeast of Boston in the New England state of Massachusetts,
C.   Plymouth, a town about 35 miles southeast of Boston in the New England, state of Massachusetts
D.   Plymouth, a town about 35 miles southeast of Boston in the New England, state of Massachusetts,
E.   Plymouth, a town about 35 miles southeast of Boston, in the New England, state of Massachusetts,

Item 15.

A.   was established by the pilgrims in December 21, 1620.
B.   was established by the pilgrims on December 21, 1620.
C.   was established by the pilgrims at December 21, 1620.
D.   was established by the pilgrims upon December 21, 1620.
E.   was established by the pilgrims during December 21, 1620.

Item 16.

    A.   Even though the early days of this new lives were filled with hope and promise,
    B.   Even though the early days of that new lives were filled with hope and promise,
    C.   Even though the early days of their new lives were filled with hope and promise,
    D.   Even though the early days of these new live were filled with hope and promise,
    E.   Even though the early days of those new live were filled with hope and promise,

Item 17.

    A.   the harsh winter proved being too much for some of the settlers.
    B.   the harsh winter proved to be too much for some of the settlers.
    C.   the harsh winter proved to being too much for some of the settlers.
    D.   the harsh winter proved been too much for some of the settlers.
    E.   the harsh winter proved to been too much for some of the settlers.

Item 18.

    A.   Near half of the pilgrims died during that first winter,
    B.   Nearly half of the pilgrims died during that first winter,
    C.   Nearly of half of the pilgrims died during that first winter,
    D.   Near of half of the pilgrims died during that first winter,
    E.   Almost near half of the pilgrims died during that first winter,

Item 19.

    A.   but those who lived go on to work hard and prosper.
    B.   but those who lived goes on to work hard and prosper.
    C.   but those who lived going on to work hard and prosper.
    D.   but those who lived went on to work hard and prosper.
    E.   but those who lived had went on to work hard and prosper.

Item 20.

Imagine that the student removed the last sentence of the essay. How would this affect the essay?

A. The essay would have a heightened emphasis on the hardships of the pilgrims.
B. The comments on the early days of the pilgrims would have increased importance.
C. The historical account of the pilgrims would lack continuity.
D. The essay would lack a sense of focus.
E. The essay would lack a proper conclusion.

Writing Test 8

Brain Waves

(*1*) <u>In 1929 that electrical activity in the human brain was first discovered.</u> (*2*) <u>Hans Berger, the German psychiatrist made the discovery,</u> (*3*) <u>was despondent to find out, in contrast to, that his research was quickly dismissed by many other scientists.</u>

(*4*) <u>The work of Berger was confirmed three years later, in 1932, when Edgar Adrian a Briton,</u> (*5*) <u>clearly demonstrated that the brain, like the heart, is profuse in its electrical activity.</u> (*6*) <u>Because of Adrian's work, it know that the electrical impulses</u> (*7*) <u>in the brain called brain waves are a mixture of four different frequencies,</u> (*8*) <u>that are based on the number of electrical impulses</u> (*9*) <u>that occurring in the brain per second.</u>

(*10*) <u>Accordingly, there are four types of brain waves as follows, alpha, beta, delta, and theta.</u> (*11*) <u>Alpha waves occur in a state of relaxation, while beta waves occur when a person is alert.</u> (*12*) <u>In addition, delta waves take place for sleep, but they can also occur dysfunctionally when the brain has been severely damaged.</u> (*13*) <u>Finally, theta waves are a</u>

frequency of *(14)* somewhere in between alpha and delta. *(15)* Seems that the purpose of theta waves is solely to facilitate the combination of the other brain waves.

(16) The whole notion of brain waves feeds into the current controversy about brain death. *(17)* Some believe that brain death is characterized by the failure of the cerebral cortex to function. *(18)* On the other hand, anothers say that mere damage to the cerebral cortex is not enough. *(19)* They assert that the brain stem function must also cease before can a person be declared dead because the cerebral cortex is responsible for other bodily processes.

Writing Test 8

Item 1.

    A.   In 1929 that electrical activity in the human brain was first discovered.
    B.   It in 1929 that electrical activity in the human brain was first discovered.
    C.   It was in 1929 that electrical activity in the human brain was first discovered.
    D.   It in 1929 was that electrical activity in the human brain was first discovered.
    E.   That in 1929 electrical activity in the human brain was first discovered.

Item 2.

    A.   Hans Berger, the German psychiatrist made the discovery,
    B.   Hans Berger, the German psychiatrist had made the discovery,
    C.   Hans Berger, the German psychiatrist who made the discovery,
    D.   Hans Berger, the German psychiatrist whom made the discovery,
    E.   Hans Berger, the German psychiatrist which made the discovery,

Item 3.

    A.   was despondent to find out, in contrast to, that his research was quickly dismissed by many other scientists.
    B.   was despondent to find out, likewise, that his research was quickly dismissed by many other scientists.
    C.   was despondent to find out, but, that his research was quickly dismissed by many other scientists.
    D.   was despondent to find out, though, that his research was quickly dismissed by many other scientists.
    E.   was despondent to find out, although, that his research was quickly dismissed by many other scientists.

Item 4.

    A.   The work of Berger was confirmed three years later, in 1932, when Edgar Adrian a Briton,
    B.   The work of Berger was confirmed three years later, in 1932, when Edgar Adrian, a Briton,
    C.   The work of Berger was confirmed three years later, in 1932, when Edgar Adrian a Briton
    D.   The work of Berger was confirmed three years later, in 1932, when Edgar Adrian a Briton;

E.   The work of Berger was confirmed three years later, in 1932, when Edgar Adrian, a Briton;

Item 5.

A.   clearly demonstrated that the brain, like the heart, is profuse in its electrical activity.
B.   demonstrated that the clearly brain, like the heart, is profuse in its electrical activity.
C.   demonstrated that the brain, like clearly the heart, is profuse in its electrical activity.
D.   demonstrated that the brain, like the heart clearly, is profuse in its electrical activity.
E.   demonstrated that the brain, like the heart, is profuse clearly in its electrical activity.

Item 6.

A.   Because of Adrian's work, it know that the electrical impulses
B.   Because of Adrian's work, it known that the electrical impulses
C.   Because of Adrian's work, it is known that the electrical impulses
D.   Because of Adrian's work, we known that the electrical impulses
E.   Because of Adrian's work, one known that the electrical impulses

Item 7.

A.   in the brain called brain waves are a mixture of four different frequencies,
B.   in the brain, called brain waves are a mixture of four different frequencies,
C.   in the brain called brain waves, are a mixture of four different frequencies,
D.   in the brain, called brain waves, are a mixture of four different frequencies,
E.   in the brain, called brain waves, are a mixture, of four different frequencies,

Item 8.

A.   that are based on the number of electrical impulses
B.   that based on the number of electrical impulses
C.   which are based on the number of electrical impulses
D.   which based on the number of electrical impulses
E.   are based on the number of electrical impulses

Item 9.

    A.   that occurring in the brain per second.
    B.   that occurred in the brain per second.
    C.   that had occurred in the brain per second.
    D.   that have occurrence in the brain per second.
    E.   that occur in the brain per second.

Item 10.

    A.   Accordingly, there are four types of brain waves as follows, alpha, beta, delta, and theta.
    B.   Accordingly, there are four types of brain waves as follows: alpha, beta, delta, and theta.
    C.   Accordingly, there are four types of brain waves as follows; alpha, beta, delta, and theta.
    D.   Accordingly, there are four types of brain waves as follows alpha, beta, delta, and theta.
    E.   Accordingly, there are four types of brain waves as follows. Alpha, beta, delta, and theta.

Item 11.

    A.   Alpha waves occur in a state of relaxation, while beta waves occur when a person is alert.
    B.   Alpha waves occur in a state of relaxation, rather beta waves occur when a person is alert.
    C.   Alpha waves occur in a state of relaxation, rather than beta waves occur when a person is alert.
    D.   Alpha waves occur in a state of relaxation, instead of waves occur when a person is alert.
    E.   Alpha waves occur in a state of relaxation, as for beta waves occur when a person is alert.

Item 12.

    A.   In addition, delta waves take place for sleep, but they can also occur dysfunctionally when the brain has been severely damaged.

    B.   In addition, delta waves take place during sleep, but they can also occur dysfunctionally when the brain has been severely damaged.

    C.   In addition, delta waves take place since sleep, but they can also occur dysfunctionally when the brain has been severely damaged.

    D.   In addition, delta waves take place with sleep, but they can also occur dysfunctionally when the brain has been severely damaged.

    E.   In addition, delta waves take place at sleep, but they can also occur dysfunctionally when the brain has been severely damaged.

Item 13.

    A.   Finally, theta waves are a frequency of

    B.   Finally, theta waves are of a frequency

    C.   Finally, theta waves of are a frequency

    D.   Finally, of theta waves are a frequency

    E.   Finally, theta waves are a of frequency

Item 14.

    A.   somewhere in between alpha and delta.

    B.   somewhere with between alpha and delta.

    C.   somewhere in besides alpha and delta.

    D.   somewhere at between alpha and delta.

    E.   somewhere at besides alpha and delta.

Item 15.

    A.   Seems that the purpose of theta waves is solely to facilitate the combination of the other brain waves.

    B.   Seemingly that the purpose of theta waves is solely to facilitate the combination of the other brain waves.

    C.   It seemingly that the purpose of theta waves is solely to facilitate the combination of the other brain waves.

    D.   It is seemingly that the purpose of theta waves is solely to facilitate the combination of the other brain waves.

    E.   It seems that the purpose of theta waves is solely to facilitate the combination of the other brain waves.

Item 16.

   A.   The whole notion of brain waves feeds into the current controversy about brain death.
   B.   The whole notion of brain waves feeds at the current controversy about brain death.
   C.   The whole notion of brain waves feeds with the current controversy about brain death.
   D.   The whole notion of brain waves feeds against the current controversy about brain death.
   E.   The whole notion of brain waves feeds for the current controversy about brain death.

Item 17.

   A.   Some believe that brain death is characterized by the failure of the cerebral cortex to function.
   B.   Some people's belief that brain death is characterized by the failure of the cerebral cortex to function.
   C.   Some peoples' belief that brain death is characterized by the failure of the cerebral cortex to function.
   D.   Certain peoples believe that brain death is characterized by the failure of the cerebral cortex to function.
   E.   Certain believe that brain death is characterized by the failure of the cerebral cortex to function.

Item 18.

   A.   On the other hand, anothers say that mere damage to the cerebral cortex is not enough.
   B.   On the other hand, another say that mere damage to the cerebral cortex is not enough.
   C.   On the other hand, others say that mere damage to the cerebral cortex is not enough.
   D.   On the other hand, other say that mere damage to the cerebral cortex is not enough.
   E.   On the other hand, other's say that mere damage to the cerebral cortex is not enough.

Item 19.

    A.   They assert that the brain stem function must also cease before can a person be declared dead because the cerebral cortex is responsible for other bodily processes.

    B.   They assert that the brain stem function must also cease before a person can be declared dead because the cerebral cortex is responsible for other bodily processes.

    C.   They assert that the brain stem function must also cease before may a person be declared dead because the cerebral cortex is responsible for other bodily processes.

    D.   They assert that the brain stem function must also cease before might a person can be declared dead because the cerebral cortex is responsible for other bodily processes.

    E.   They assert that the brain stem function must also cease before a person declared dead because the cerebral cortex is responsible for other bodily processes.

Item 20.

Imagine that the student would like to add the following sentence to the essay. What is the best location for this sentence?

Therefore, for these myriad reasons, it has become very important to measure brain activity.

    A.   At the end of the first paragraph.
    B.   At the end of the second paragraph.
    C.   At the end of the third paragraph.
    D.   At the beginning of the last paragraph.
    E.   At the end of the last paragraph.

Writing Test 9

The Middle Ages

(*1*) <u>The Middle Ages period were a time of significant social and political change.</u>

(*2*) <u>Even though the Germanic invasion in the fifth century,</u> (*3*) <u>the autocratic system of Roman government had overthrown.</u> (*4*) <u>In that place today is a collection of independent democratic nations.</u> (*5*) <u>However, this development would not have been possible whether its foundations had not been laid throughout the Middle Ages.</u>

(*6*) <u>Indeed, a productive process lay beneath many seemingly everyday, bantering activities during this era.</u> (*7*) <u>New societies began to materialize as for the German invaders became acquainted with the Roman inhabitants.</u> (*8*) <u>This intermingling of nationalities and ethnic groups was an important process, that should not be overlooked</u> (*9*) <u>because those type of hybridity bears</u> (*10*) <u>a great deal of resemblance with the ethnic diversity of certain communities in modern society.</u>

(*11*) Nevertheless, economic layers was still present at this time. (*12*) Many of the warriors invading had established themselves as affluent farmers. (*13*) It's wealth was in stark contrast to the life of the lower class slaves and peasants, (*14*) who often had large families.

(*15*) In addition, this period witnessed the rise in imperialism, defined as a political system for which a king or queen has absolute power. (*16*) While many kings strived to rule in accordance with the law, some rulers treated their citizens harshly, without establishing followed legal restrictions.

(*17*) Yet, their appalling living conditions, the common populace began to challenge the imperial system during the Middle Ages. (*18*) Changing the attitudes of people towards their rulers, (*19*) the balance of power in the political system also began to have shift.

(*20*) To a significant, extent these challenges influenced the functioning of present-day political systems.

Writing Test 9

Item 1.

A. The Middle Ages period were a time of significant social and political change.
B. The Middle Ages period was a time of significant social and political change.
C. The Middle Age's period were a time of significant social and political change.
D. The Middle Age's period was a time of significant social and political change.
E. The Middle Ages period, it was a time of significant social and political change.

Item 2.

A. Even though the Germanic invasion in the fifth century,
B. Despite of the Germanic invasion in the fifth century,
C. As a result of the Germanic invasion in the fifth century,
D. In effect, the Germanic invasion in the fifth century,
E. For the reason of the Germanic invasion in the fifth century,

Item 3.

A. the autocratic system of Roman government had overthrown.
B. the autocratic system of Roman government have overthrown.
C. the autocratic system of Roman government to have overthrown.
D. the autocratic system of Roman government was overthrown.
E. the autocratic system of Roman government was being overthrown.

Item 4.

A. In that place today is a collection of independent democratic nations.
B. In it's place today is a collection of independent democratic nations.
C. In its place today is a collection of independent democratic nations.
D. In our place today is a collection of independent democratic nations.
E. In one's place today is a collection of independent democratic nations.

Item 5.

    A.   However, this development would not have been possible whether its foundations had not been laid throughout the Middle Ages.

    B.   However, this development would not have been possible whenever its foundations had not been laid throughout the Middle Ages.

    C.   However, this development would not have been possible whether its foundations were not been lain throughout the Middle Ages.

    D.   However, this development would not have been possible if its foundations were not layed throughout the Middle Ages.

    E.   However, this development would not have been possible if its foundations had not been laid throughout the Middle Ages.

Item 6.

    A.   Indeed, a productive process lay beneath many seemingly everyday, bantering activities during this era.

    B.   Indeed, a productive process lay beneath many seemingly everyday, benign activities during this era.

    C.   Indeed, a productive process lay beneath many seemingly everyday, bogus activities during this era.

    D.   Indeed, a productive process lay beneath many seemingly everyday, banal activities during this era.

    E.   Indeed, a productive process lay beneath many seemingly everyday, borderline activities during this era.

Item 7.

    A.   New societies began to materialize as for the German invaders became acquainted with the Roman inhabitants.

    B.   New societies began to materialize as when the German invaders became acquainted with the Roman inhabitants.

    C.   New societies began to materialize as than the German invaders became acquainted with the Roman inhabitants.

    D.   New societies began to materialize as while the German invaders became acquainted with the Roman inhabitants.

    E.   New societies began to materialize as the German invaders became acquainted with the Roman inhabitants.

Item 8.

- A.   This intermingling of nationalities and ethnic groups was an important process, that should not be overlooked
- B.   This intermingling of nationalities and ethnic groups was an important process. That should not be overlooked
- C.   This intermingling of nationalities and ethnic groups was an important process that should not be overlooked
- D.   This intermingling of nationalities and ethnic groups was an important process one should not be overlooked
- E.   This intermingling of nationalities and ethnic groups was an important process, one should not be overlooked

Item 9.

- A.   because those type of hybridity bears
- B.   because these type of hybridity bears
- C.   because this type of hybridity bears
- D.   because this types of hybridity bears
- E.   because that types of hybridity bears

Item 10.

- A.   a great deal of resemblance with the ethnic diversity of certain communities in modern society.
- B.   a great deal of resemblance to the ethnic diversity of certain communities in modern society.
- C.   a great deal of resemblance for the ethnic diversity of certain communities in modern society.
- D.   a great deal of resemblance like the ethnic diversity of certain communities in modern society.
- E.   a great deal of resemblance such as to the ethnic diversity of certain communities in modern society.

Item 11.

    A.   Nevertheless, economic layers was still present at this time.
    B.   Nevertheless, economic layering was still present at this time.
    C.   Nevertheless, economic stratification was still present at this time.
    D.   Nevertheless, economic strata was still present at this time.
    E.   Nevertheless, economic stratum were still present at this time.

Item 12.

    A.   Many of the warriors invading had established themselves as affluent farmers.
    B.   Many of the warriors had established invading themselves as affluent farmers.
    C.   Many of the warriors had established themselves invading as affluent farmers.
    D.   Many of the invading warriors had established themselves as affluent farmers.
    E.   Invading many of the warriors had established themselves as affluent farmers.

Item 13.

    A.   It's wealth was in stark contrast to the life of the lower class slaves and peasants,
    B.   Its wealth was in stark contrast to the life of the lower class slaves and peasants,
    C.   Their wealth was in stark contrast to the life of the lower class slaves and peasants,
    D.   The wealth of their's was in stark contrast to the life of the lower class slaves and peasants,
    E.   The wealth of theirs' was in stark contrast to the life of the lower class slaves and peasants,

Item 14.

    A.   who often had large families.
    B.   who often lived with their families.
    C.   who often lived in extremely poor conditions.
    D.   who were often born and working in the countryside.
    E.   who were often living and working in the countryside.

Item 15.

    A.   In addition, this period witnessed the rise in imperialism, defined as a political system for which a king or queen has absolute power.

    B.   In addition, this period witnessed the rise in imperialism, defined as a political system in which a king or queen has absolute power.

    C.   In addition, this period witnessed the rise in imperialism, defined as a political system which a king or queen has absolute power.

    D.   In addition, this period witnessed the rise in imperialism, defined as a political system, which a king or queen has absolute power.

    E.   In addition, this period witnessed the rise in imperialism, defined as a political system that a king or queen has absolute power.

Item 16.

    A.   While many kings strived to rule in accordance with the law, some rulers treated their citizens harshly, without establishing followed legal restrictions.

    B.   While many kings strived to rule in accordance with the law, some rulers treated their citizens harshly, without followed establishing legal restrictions.

    C.   While many kings strived to rule in accordance with the law, some rulers treated their citizens harshly, without following established legal restrictions.

    D.   While many kings strived to rule in accordance with the law, some rulers treated their citizens harshly, without legal following established restrictions.

    E.   While many kings strived to rule in accordance with the law, some rulers treated their citizens harshly, without legal establishing followed restrictions.

Item 17.

    A.   Yet, their appalling living conditions, the common populace began to challenge the imperial system during the Middle Ages.

    B.   Yet, in spite their appalling living conditions, the common populace began to challenge the imperial system during the Middle Ages.

    C.   Yet, despite their appalling living conditions, the common populace began to challenge the imperial system during the Middle Ages.

    D.   Yet, although their appalling living conditions, the common populace began to challenge the imperial system during the Middle Ages.

    E.   Yet, whereas their appalling living conditions, the common populace began to challenge the imperial system during the Middle Ages.

Item 18.

    A.   Changing the attitudes of people towards their rulers,
    B.   As changing as the attitudes of people towards their rulers,
    C.   As the attitudes of people towards their rulers changed,
    D.   As changed the attitudes of people towards their rulers,
    E.   Had changed the attitudes of people towards their rulers,

Item 19.

    A.   the balance of power in the political system also began to have shift.
    B.   the balance of power in the political system also began to had shift.
    C.   the balance of power in the political system also began to had shifted.
    D.   the balance of power in the political system also began to shifting.
    E.   the balance of power in the political system also began to shift.

Item 20.

    A.   To a significant extent, these challenges influenced the functioning of present-day political systems.
    B.   To a significant extent these challenges, influenced the functioning of present-day political systems.
    C.   To a significant extent these challenges influenced, the functioning of present-day political systems.
    D.   To a significant extent these challenges influenced the functioning, of present-day political systems.
    E.   To a significant extent these challenges, influenced the functioning, of present-day political systems.

Item 21.

Suppose the purpose of this assignment was to explain how the Middle Ages affected present day political systems. Has the student achieved this purpose?

    A.   No, because the student has not given a detailed explanation of the functioning of modern-day political systems.

    B.   No, because the student has not sufficiently related aspects of the Middle Age system to the present day politics.

    C.   No, because the essay lacks clear examples and a persuasive line of reasoning.

    D.   Yes, because the student has mentioned the effect of the Middle Ages on present-day democracy, as well as its relationship with multi-ethnicity.

    E.   Yes, because the student has enumerated similarities between aspects of the Roman government with those of the present day.

Writing Test 10

Cancer Risk

(*1*) <u>Cancer, a group of mainly than 100 different types of disease,</u> (*2*) <u>occurs where</u> <u>cells in the body begin to divide abnormally and continue dividing and forming more cells</u> <u>without control or order.</u> (*3*) <u>All internal organs of the body consist of cells, which normally</u> <u>divide to produce more cells when the body requires them.</u> (*4*) <u>This is a natural, orderly</u> <u>process, that keeps human beings healthy.</u>

(*5*) <u>If a cell divides when is not necessary, a large growth called a tumor can form.</u>

(*6*) <u>These tumors can usually be removed, and in many cases, they do not recurrence.</u> (*7*) <u>Unfortunately, in some cases the cancer at the original tumor spreads.</u> (*8*) <u>The spread of</u> <u>cancer in such way is called metastasis.</u>

(*9*) <u>There are some factors which are being known to increase the risk of cancer.</u>

(*10*) <u>Smoking is the single cause largest of death from cancer in the United States.</u> (*11*) <u>One-</u> <u>third of the death's from cancer each year are related to smoking,</u> (*12*) <u>making tobacco use the</u> <u>most preventable cause of death in this country.</u>

(13) Choice of food can also be link to cancer.   *(14)* Research shows that there are a

link between high-fat food and certain cancers, and being seriously overweight is also a cancer

risk.   *(15)* Cancer risk can be reduced with a cut down on fatty food and eating generous

amounts of fruit and vegetables.

Writing Test 10

Item 1.

    A.   Cancer, a group of mainly than 100 different types of disease,
    B.   Cancer, a group of more than 100 different types of disease,
    C.   Cancer, a group of 100 more different types of disease,
    D.   Cancer, a group of mostly than 100 different types of disease,
    E.   Cancer, a group of almost than 100 different types of disease,

Item 2.

    A.   occurs where cells in the body begin to divide abnormally and continue dividing and forming more cells without control or order.
    B.   occurs which cells in the body begin to divide abnormally and continue dividing and forming more cells without control or order.
    C.   occurs in which cells in the body begin to divide abnormally and continue dividing and forming more cells without control or order.
    D.   occurs when cells in the body begin to divide abnormally and continue dividing and forming more cells without control or order.
    E.   occurs once when cells in the body begin to divide abnormally and continue dividing and forming more cells without control or order.

Item 3.

    A.   All internal organs of the body consist of cells, which normally divide to produce more cells when the body requires them.
    B.   All internal organs of the body consist of cells, which divide to normally produce more cells when the body requires them.
    C.   All internal organs of the body consist of cells, which divide to produce more normally cells when the body requires them.
    D.   All internal organs of the body consist of cells, which divide to produce more cells when normally the body requires them.
    E.   All internal organs of the body consist of cells, which divide to produce more cells when the body requires them normally.

Item 4.

    A.   This is a natural, orderly process, that keeps human beings healthy.
    B.   This is a natural, orderly process that keeps human beings healthy.
    C.   This is a natural orderly process, that keeps human beings healthy.
    D.   This is a natural orderly process that keeps human beings healthy.
    E.   This is a natural orderly, process that keeps human beings healthy.

Item 5.

    A.   If a cell divides when is not necessary, a large growth called a tumor can form.
    B.   If a cell divides when they are not necessary, a large growth called a tumor can form.
    C.   If a cell divides when it is not necessary, a large growth called a tumor can form.
    D.   If a cell divides when are not necessary, a large growth called a tumor can form.
    E.   If a cell divides when that not necessary, a large growth called a tumor can form.

Item 6.

    A.   These tumors can usually be removed, and in many cases, they do not recurrence.
    B.   These tumors can usually be removed, and in many cases, they do not make recurrence.
    C.   These tumors can usually be removed, and in many cases, they do not recurring.
    D.   These tumors can usually be removed, and in many cases, they do not are recurred.
    E.   These tumors can usually be removed, and in many cases, they do not recur.

Item 7.

    A.   Unfortunately, in some cases the cancer at the original tumor spreads.
    B.   Unfortunately, in some cases the cancer from the original tumor spreads.
    C.   Unfortunately, in some cases the cancer with the original tumor spreads.
    D.   Unfortunately, in some cases the cancer for the original tumor spreads.
    E.   Unfortunately, in some cases the cancer below the original tumor spreads.

Item 8.

A.   The spread of cancer in such way is called metastasis.
B.   The spread of cancer in such a way is called metastasis.
C.   The spread of cancer in such ways is called metastasis.
D.   The spread of cancer in such like way is called metastasis.
E.   The spread of cancer in such like ways is called metastasis.

Item 9.

A.   There are some factors which are being known to increase the risk of cancer.
B.   There are some factors which are know to increase the risk of cancer.
C.   There are some factors which are knowing to increase the risk of cancer.
D.   There are some factors which are known to increase the risk of cancer.
E.   There are some factors which have known to increase the risk of cancer.

Item.10

A.   Smoking is the single cause largest of death from cancer in the United States.
B.   Smoking is the single cause of largest death from cancer in the United States.
C.   Smoking is the single cause of death largest from cancer in the United States.
D.   Smoking is the single cause of death from cancer largest in the United States.
E.   Smoking is the largest single cause of death from cancer in the United States.

Item 11.

A.   One-third of the death's from cancer each year are related to smoking,
B.   One-third of the deaths' from cancer each year are related to smoking,
C.   One-third of the deaths from cancer each year are related to smoking,
D.   One-third of cancer's deaths each year are related to smoking,
E.   One-third of cancers' deaths each year are related to smoking,

Item 12.

    A.   making tobacco use the most preventable cause of death in this country.

    B.   which making tobacco use the most preventable cause of death in this country.

    C.   made tobacco use the most preventable cause of death in this country.

    D.   which will be making tobacco use the most preventable cause of death in this country.

    E.   in making tobacco use the most preventable cause of death in this country.

Item 13.

    A.   Choice of food can also be link to cancer.

    B.   Choice of food can also be linking to cancer.

    C.   Choice of food can also be linked to cancer.

    D.   Choice of food can also been linked to cancer.

    E.   Choice of food can also link to cancer.

Item 14.

    A.   Research shows that there are a link between high-fat food and certain cancers, and being seriously overweight is also a cancer risk.

    B.   Research shows that there is a link between high-fat food and certain cancers, and being seriously overweight is also a cancer risk.

    C.   Research shows that there's links between high-fat food and certain cancers, and being seriously overweight is also a cancer risk.

    D.   Research shows that there is existing a link between high-fat food and certain cancers, and being seriously overweight is also a cancer risk.

    E.   Research shows that there in existence a link between high-fat food and certain cancers, and being seriously overweight is also a cancer risk.

Item 15.

    A.   Cancer risk can be reduced with a cut down on fatty food and eating generous amounts of fruit and vegetables.

    B.   Cancer risk can be reduced with cutting down on fatty food and eating generous amounts of fruit and vegetables.

    C.   Cancer risk can be reduced with cutting down fatty food and eating generous amounts of fruit and vegetables.

    D.   Cancer risk can be reduced by cutting down on fatty food and eating generous amounts of fruit and vegetables.

    E.   Cancer risk can be reduced by cut down on fatty food and eating generous amounts of fruit and vegetables.

Item 16.

Suppose the student wants to include an admonition to the reader about how he or she can prevent cancer risks. Which sentence, if added to the end of the essay, would achieve this purpose?

    A.   Accordingly, the government needs to act now to help improve the health of the country.

    B.   In these circumstances, militating against the causes of cancer is bound to be a difficult but necessary task.

    C.   It is therefore the responsibility of each individual to try to mitigate cancer risk by living a more healthy lifestyle.

    D.   However, these deaths could easily have been avoided.

    E.   Nevertheless, most people agree that trying to prevent cancer risk is extremely important.

ANSWERS

Writing Test 1

1) E
2) A
3) B
4) B
5) D
6) A
7) B
8) B
9) B
10) B
11) C
12) B
13) B
14) C
15) C
16) A
17) E
18) C
19) A
20) B
21) C
22) D

Writing Test 2

1) A
2) B
3) D
4) D
5) B
6) B
7) D
8) A
9) C
10) B
11) B
12) A

13) C
14) A
15) D
16) B
17) B
18) B
19) D
20) C
21) D
22) D

Writing Test 3

1) D
2) A
3) E
4) C
5) B
6) A
7) B
8) C
9) C
10) C
11) E
12) E
13) B
14) C
15) B
16) C
17) A
18) D
19) B
20) B
21) D
22) B

Writing Test 4

1) C
2) B
3) D

4) E
5) E
6) E
7) C
8) B
9) A
10) B
11) C
12) B
13) C
14) E
15) B
16) D

Writing Test 5

1) B
2) C
3) D
4) C
5) A
6) B
7) B
8) B
9) D
10) C
11) A
12) B
13) C
14) B
15) B
16) E
17) C
18) B
19) D
20) E

Writing Test 6

1) D
2) B
3) A
4) E
5) B
6) C
7) D
8) B
9) C
10) B
11) C
12) B
13) D
14) C
15) E
16) D
17) C
18) B
19) A
20) D
21) E

Writing Test 7

1) C
2) D
3) D
4) D
5) C
6) E
7) C
8) B
9) E
10) B
11) A
12) D
13) C
14) B
15) B

16) C
17) B
18) B
19) D
20) E

Writing Test 8

1) C
2) C
3) D
4) B
5) A
6) C
7) D
8) C
9) E
10) B
11) A
12) B
13) B
14) A
15) E
16) A
17) A
18) C
19) B
20) E

Writing Test 9

1) B
2) C
3) D
4) C
5) E
6) D
7) E
8) C
9) C
10) B

11) C
12) D
13) C
14) C
15) B
16) C
17) C
18) C
19) E
20) A
21) B

Writing Test 10

1) B
2) D
3) A
4) B
5) C
6) E
7) B
8) B
9) D
10) E
11) C
12) A
13) C
14) B
15) D
16) C

9211433R0

Made in the USA
Lexington, KY
07 April 2011